MW01093404

THOUGHT CATALOG BOOKS

Fiercely Independent (Most Days)

Fiercely Independent (Most Days)

MARISA DONNELLY

THOUGHT CATALOG BOOKS

Brooklyn, NY

THOUGHT CATALOG BOOKS

Copyright © 2016 by The Thought & Expression Co.

All rights reserved. Published by Thought Catalog Books, a division of The Thought & Expression Co., Williamsburg, Brooklyn. Founded in 2010, Thought Catalog is a website and imprint dedicated to your ideas and stories. We publish fiction and non-fiction from emerging and established writers across all genres. For general information and submissions: manuscripts@thoughtcatalog.com.

First edition, 2016

ISBN 978-1530388110

10 9 8 7 6 5 4 3 2 1

Cover photography by © Jay Mantri

Contents

1

I Have No Interest In Being The 'Right' Kind Of Woman

I don't need you to tell me who I am, who I need to be, what kind of woman I should become.

I love my long, curly hair. I love the birthmark on my cheek. I love the chicken pox scar on my belly. I love the rough patch of skin on my middle finger, a writer's curse.

I love my Midwest twang, the way I always walk with a purpose, the fact that I am continually doing 65 things at once. That is the person I am.

And I am proud of her.

I am a woman. And whatever shape that should be, I don't care. I do not need to fit this female mold, the 'should be,' 'supposed to be,' 'right' kind of woman.

I have no interest in being the right kind of woman.

I don't need you to tell me that I should dress my age, that I need to grow up, that my belly button ring is suggestive.

I don't need you to tell me that heels are for girls that are 'asking for it' and that drinking wine from the bottle isn't classy.

I don't need you to tell me that I should stop lifting weights because a girl that's too muscular isn't attractive. I don't need you to shake your head at my legs. Tell me they're too thick, too strong.

A strong woman is a feared woman. I hope your knees shake when you see me.

I am a woman of words, a woman of thoughts, a woman of plans. I know where I'm going and I'll get there my way. My choice. My decision.

I don't need your approval to be the woman I want to be, the woman I am.

I don't need you to tell me where I should live, what I should spend my money on, who I should love. I don't need you to tell me that you know me better than anyone else. Because you don't.

I know myself.

And I know that I love my baby face. I love my muscular calves. I love my open, but strong heart.

And I don't need your approval for who I am.

I don't need you.

2

You Won't Find Yourself Unless You Allow Yourself To Be Selfish

You are twenty-two, my heart tells me, *you have dreams to chase, regrets to make, challenges to face, people to fall in love with, and memories to create.*

I *am* twenty-two. And if there's something the last five months have taught me—as I transition from a college graduate to a full-time employee, as I move out of my parents' house, as I pay for bills and file my taxes and cook my own meals and navigate a completely unknown future—it's that it is perfectly okay to be selfish.

To know what I want and what I deserve. To make dreams, tiny and manageable or giant and unrealistic. To lay out plans and wishes and hopes. To get up early, to stay out late, to binge-watch Netflix, to spend all afternoon at the gym, to get drunk on a Monday, to fall asleep before 9PM. To eliminate negative people and surround myself with happiness. To forgive.

Right now is the time in my life to make decisions. For myself. To stop worrying about what my mother, aunt, significant other, best friend in the entire world, or ex thinks about what I'm doing.

The time to let go of my self-hate, my anger, my resentment for others and focus on myself. *What makes me happy? What is important to me? What do I want? What do I need?*

"Selfish" has always been a dirty word. You are selfish. That means you put yourself first. That means you don't care about anyone but yourself. But is that such a bad thing?

To be selfish means to know who you are as a person and what you need. It means taking the time to do things that you want to do. It means not changing your plans, your thoughts, your words, your actions, yourself for the sake of someone else. Sure, it means you potentially have the power to hurt others, but this is an unintentional part of the process of becoming you, becoming whole.

It is awesome to be selfish. To stop over-thinking, over-analyzing, questioning every decision you make. When you are selfish, you give yourself the opportunity to grow. You do things solely because you feel compelled to. You chase your emotions, you follow what your heart and head are telling you. And most importantly, you do things because you want to, not because you are told.

It is healthy to be selfish. To decide, for yourself, that you want to spend the day exploring nature, napping all afternoon, or partying until 3AM. You allow your mind and your body to connect and do something that you want to do, free of distractions, fears, inhibitions, and regrets.

So as I sit in a quiet library, watching snowflakes press their miniature selves against the windows and wishing for something more, I remind myself that it's okay to be selfish, to take the world, swallow it whole, and claim it as my own.

3

This Is How You Embrace Change

You don't, at first.

You fight it because you're human, because you're used to the world and the way it is, because you're terrified. You fight change because you've been told that change is scary, that change is difficult, that change hurts.

You've learned that sometimes it's easier to stay in one place and accept rather than to do or say something different, than to move, than to become something else. All this is understandable. You've set a routine, you're comfortable, complacent. But that is the best part about change, it fights against complacency. It makes you grow.

At first you don't accept change. You can't. But then you start, little by little, like a big toe dipped into the pool water. You see things in a new light for the first time, you become a little less terrified, a little less stuck in your ways.

You take baby steps. In small ways, you begin to embrace that your life is moving in a direction you never thought it would. You take each day, each hour as it comes. You breathe deeply. You remind yourself of who you have been, who you are. You remind yourself that despite the world swirling around you, you will still be that person, only stronger.

You find things that make you laugh. You remind yourself again and again that you still have the ability to laugh. No matter how upside-down your life is, you can still laugh. That is a blessing.

You close your eyes and you love more. You learn to forgive, to let go of what you cannot control. You think deeper. You remind yourself of the good you've had, the good you will have. You love—people, places, memories, things, adventures. You open your heart, slowly, peeking out from your shell and you see the world as something new. You see change as an opportunity and less of a roadblock. You realize, that no, life is not over. You are just beginning, again. Moving forward, circling, becoming new.

You acknowledge that this is part of the process. That life will never stay the same, but will always be growing, shifting, orbiting the sun bringing day and night. You know that life will have its consistencies, but that it is ultimately always moving. And you decide to accept this.

Then you begin to embrace change whole-heartedly. You smile in the face of fear. You make the conscious choice to say, yes. To say, this is change and this is okay.

And your life begins to shift more easily. You lessen the reins on what you simply cannot hold onto. You lean into the hope that what is coming will pave itself out, an open road ready for you to drive on, to take whatever curves and bends and backroads you choose. And you trust in the fact that change is indeed necessary, a part of your journey. It is this change that leads you, strengthens you, balances you, and molds you into the person you are. And this is good.

4

I Am Not The Type Of Woman You Can Push Around

This is what you need to know about me: I'll love the hell out of you. I'll care for you. But I'll be damned if you think I'm the woman that will sit silently next to you, that will do everything for you, pick up after you, be your mother. That's not me.

I am a bed-hogging, heel-wearing, feisty kind of woman. I'm the kind of woman who will stand up to you when you're not treating me right, that will challenge you, that will steal your half of the covers.

When the world pushes against me, I'll push back. I'll come fighting with fists and words and muscles and heart. That's how I've been raised; that's how I fought through when no one thought I could.

I will never be the kind of woman that sits down and shuts up. The kind of woman that waits back and lets her man always be the driver, the hand that leads her across the room, the voice that tells her what to do, who to be. That will never be me.

If you're looking for a trophy wife, for someone to sit and

smile complacently at your side, for someone to be your mother and keep you in line, I'm not her. I'll love you, but I won't take your sh*t. I'll be honest with you. I will stand up to you, and I will stand in spite of you. But I will also stand for you.

This is who I'll be: When push comes to shove, I'll be the woman fighting alongside you. The woman with hands that can heal. The woman who will love you with the sweetest tenderness, but will fight like hell against a world that tries to control her. I'll be your mess of curly hair and fierce emotions. I'll be your fighter. I'll be your partner, your other half, your go-to, your equal. I'll be the woman you love. And we'll conquer this world together, side by side.

5

I Have A Girly-Girl Side And I'm Not Afraid To Own It

You're such a girl, my guy friend says to me as I point out a pair of adorable, fluffy deer scampering across the small-town road and call them 'cute.' (They *were* totally cute, by the way).

This isn't the first time I've heard that phrase. I was 'such a girl' when I spent time in front of the stacks of throw pillows at Target, debating between a chevron print and a tribal pattern. I was 'such a girl' for ordering a Twisted Berry Mojito at Buffalo Wild Wings. I was 'such a girl' for getting my car stuck in a snow bank and needing another pair of hands to push.

This phrase was casual. Maybe an insult, but more likely a tease. A seemingly-harmless line my guy friends threw out there just to poke fun at my 'feminine' traits.

But being 'such a girl' doesn't bother me. I don't take it as an insult. Actually, I love being a girl.

I love putting on makeup. Or not. I love doing my hair. Or throwing it in a messy bun. I love dressing up. Or dressing down.

I love shopping. But I hate it some days. I love talking about life with my girls. But I also like kicking it with the guys and discussing the score of the last Blackhawks game.

I'm 'such a girl.'

Yes, I think furry animals are cute. There's no shame in that. (Because they are). And I'll spend all the time I want in front of the frilly throw pillows and other cutesy items because I want my house to look homey. (Guys act like they don't notice these things…but they totally do. And if they don't, who cares?)

I'll order the fruitiest drink on the menu, but then I'll get just as many wings as the guys. And eat them. And make a mess. And lick my fingers clean. (No shame. Food's good.)

I'll put on a cocktail dress and jewelry. But you better believe I'll rock a good pair of sweats and Nikes, too.

You can find me dancing in my heels, but you'll also find me at the gym.

And by the way, I *do* throw like a girl. A collegiate softball starting pitcher type of girl.

Yes, I'm 'such a girl.' I might get my car stuck in a snowbank (once in a blue moon) but I'll be right next to the guys pushing it out. I might need help sometimes, but I most definitely have my sh*t together 99% of the time.

I *am* such a girl. A cute and feminine, but tough and head-strong girl. And no, that's not an insult.

6

This Is How You Are Keeping Yourself From The Beautiful Life You Deserve (And How To Change)

This is how you keep yourself from happiness:

First, begin your day with worry. Open your eyes and check your phone. Agonize over the texts and you did or didn't get. Watch all the Snapstories you missed out on. Wonder if he or she is still mad at you, whether you should have made other plans last night, or what you're going to do today but make no forward motion. Stay still, static, and angry.

Then, start to overthink. Tell yourself you shouldn't drink that coffee because it has too many calories. Imagine your future spring break body and shame yourself. Put on comfy sweats, then take them off because they're too lazy-looking. Shimmy on your fancy jeans, then wonder if it looks like you're trying too hard. Take a selfie. Post it. Then quickly delete it in embarrassment.

Start to stress. Stress over your busy schedule or lack thereof. Or what you should be doing vs. what you are doing. Tell yourself that you're not enough, that you're a mess, that you need to get your life together. Tell yourself that you're never going to figure it out, that happiness will always be just out of reach.

Go about your day expecting the worst, holding onto grudges and anxiety and fear. Dwell in the negative corners of your mind and push other people away. Restrict yourself from doing what you want for whatever excuse or reason. Withdraw inside your angry self and stay there, brooding.

Don't take the steps to change your mindset. Don't try to improve. Don't let love bless your life. Continue on the same, sh*tty road and refuse to let go. Convince yourself that you can fix what you simply can't. Exhaust yourself trying to change what can't be changed. Then feel even more discouraged, and let this consume you.

Before you go to bed, check your phone and fill your mind with angry thoughts. Choose not to forgive, choose not to release your tight grip on what you can't control. Go to sleep with negative voices in your head. And believe that this is how it's always going to be.

———

But guess what? **This is not how it's always going to be.** Unless you let it. Unless you keep yourself covered and burdened and suffocated and choked by negativity. Unless you break away from the things that drive you crazy and bring you down, and say, *I'm done. I'm tired of holding myself back from a good life.*

Then, suddenly, you lift the sheet from your face and see the world as it truly is—imperfect, broken, confusing, wonderful, breath-taking, terrifying, messy—and despite the pain, despite the awful parts, and despite every negative fiber pushing against your ribcage, trying to shove its way into your heart, choose to see the positive.

Choose to change your perspective; change your world. And live the life of happiness you have always deserved.

7

I Am Not A 'Netflix And Chill' Kind Of Girl

I am not just a 'Netflix and Chill' kind of girl. Not the *Hey babe, come over now that it's 3AM and I'm bored and lonely.* Not the *close the door and make-out with me during this entire movie.* Not the *let's sit and watch thirty-five back-to-back episodes of* Orange is the New Black *and share this box of pizza* type. No.

I am the kind of girl that wants you to take me on a crazy adventure... to the backyard. Push me on the tree swing and tell me about your life, your hometown, your high school best friend. Let's take a walk around the block. Let's skip rocks on the pond. Let's get in your car and go to a playground, take turns sliding down the slides. Let's just play music and drive.

Entertain my mind. Tell me something that makes you happy, like when you hit that two-run triple that won the state championship or when you taught your little brother how to fish. Let's build a campfire. Let's play cards, write a bucket list, compare or the size of our big toes. Take me somewhere. On a vacation. A trip to South Beach, a flight to Miami for Ultra Music Festival, a ticket to the Minnesota State Fair. Spoil me. But not always. I'm not a needy girl.

Take me to the little hole-in-the-wall Chinese restaurant on 53rd and James. To the drive in movie theatre thirty miles out of town. I want adventures with you. I want memories. I want us to look back through albums of pictures, me on your lap, your one hand on my hip and the other pointing to the photograph of us on the ledge of the Grand Canyon, my smile stretched across my face like a little kid's.

I don't want your money. Not always. I really just want your time. I don't mind cuddling on the couch for a movie. And I don't mind pizza, especially when it's pepperoni, sausage, and onion, but I don't want the same routine. I don't want the TV over the sound of your voice.

Some days I am content just lying next to you. Not saying anything. Just feeling your heartbeat and mine, letting my mind wander to future dates, future memories, future adventures. I don't always want something crazy. Some nights I just want to be around you and friends, laughing and throwing back beers.

I'm not the kind of girl you can call when you're lonely. The girl you know you can text and she'll always pick up. The girl that you can hold until you fall asleep then do the same thing tomorrow. The girl who will just sit and watch shows with you, day after day, night after night.No, I'm not just a 'Netflix and chill' type of girl. I want to hear about the little things that make you, you. Your biggest regret, how dandelions make your nose itchy, that your favorite season is fall, or the time you broke your toe riding your best friend's bicycle in fuzzy slippers.

I want you to challenge me. Change my view on politics, on religion. Teach me how to fix a flat tire, how to say 'hello' in six different languages, how to dribble a soccer ball.

I don't want to be bored by you. I want to spend my life making adventures with you. Carving our initials into tree bark and mountain sides, buying fifty-cent post cards from every gas station in the U.S. and mailing them to ourselves, trying beer in every country, collecting sand from each beach we've walked on.

I want to go to bed every night exhausted. Wake up every morning renewed. I want to chase dreams with you. I want to be the reason you feel young, the reason you love life. I want to be more than just the girl you've seen every television episode with.

Don't get me wrong. I will watch movies with you, a bucket of caramel corn between us, my head snuggled against your chest, our legs intertwined. I will build forts in the living room, dress in my comfiest baggy clothes, have marathons of Breaking Bad and consume copious amounts of junk food. These things will make me happy, too. But not as exciting as living our lives. Not the same as sharing memories and moments as good—even better—than what's on the television screen.

8

20 Small Ways You Can Love Yourself A Little More Each Morning

1. Look in the mirror and find one thing that makes you unique.

2. Compliment yourself as you brush your teeth—a compliment about a physical aspect, and a compliment about your personality.

3. Give yourself a few extra minutes so you're not racing to get ready.

4. Smile, at your reflection.

5. Smile, just because.

6. Put on an outfit that makes you feel good.

7. Breathe deeply.

8. Listen to your favorite song as you get ready.

9. Take a few extra minutes to put on lotion on, or paint your nails.

10. Wear a cute piece of jewelry that you haven't before.

11. Put on makeup, or don't.

12. Tell yourself that you are confident.

13. Fill your mind with positive thoughts.

14. Take a moment to make yourself coffee, hot chocolate, a super healthy smoothie to start off the day.

15. Take a selfie and post it, or keep it for yourself.

16. Put on your favorite perfume.

17. Read a motivational quote.

18. Start your car so you have a comfortable ride to work.

19. Plan one fun thing to do for yourself later in the day.

20. Tell yourself you're going to have a good day. Then do just that.

9

You Are Not A 'Squad Goals' Type Of Girl

You are not the girl with the tight dress and eyebrow game on point. You are not the girl surrounded by her perfect friends with perfect shades of eyeshadow and perfect smiles and perfect teeth.

You are not the girl that stands in the back of the photo with a red lipstick smile and the identical black miniskirt and flowy top. Who holds her best friend's hand, who makes kissy faces, who is always surrounded by her other attractive friends, who travels to the bathroom in packs.

You are not the girl who calls her best friend before the party and asks what to wear, who goes to the mall with several others, who reads the group text religiously to know what she's doing with her Saturday afternoon.

Nope. You are not the 'Squad Goals' type.

You are the girl that can do things herself. Who wakes up and pulls on that oversized hoodie and jeans, or sundress, or shorts and a tank-top. Or whatever the hell you want. Because you really don't care what anyone else thinks and it's your decision.

You go to the library. To the gym. To the city park. To the farmer's market and spend the morning sniffing strawberries. You don't need a group around you. A group of girls to tell you that your makeup is perfect, that your hair is parted the way it should be, that you're wearing the 'right' clothes. You don't have to fit in, be surrounded by everyone else who looks the same, has the same thoughts. You are just you.

You are the girl that gets on a subway train and wanders around the city. You walk without a map. You ignore everyone's suggestions and just do your own thing. You aren't naïve. You just aren't afraid to do things alone. You trust yourself. You're confident. And so you face the world solo.

You don't feel the need to fit in the little box. The little box of 'cute,' of 'sexy,' of 'dateable' of 'best friend' of 'perfect'. You stick your tongue out in pictures. You ditch the pictures all together. You don't have to be the friend in the back row in a matching outfit. And you aren't that friend.

You love yourself. And that's okay. It's okay not to spend your days worrying about what your girlfriends think, not to immerse yourself in their thoughts and group pictures, not to wear color-coordinated dresses. You have friends and you love them. But you aren't defined by them.

It's okay to wake up and do what you want. To shop by yourself. To travel solo. To run the gravel path around your neighborhood alone. It's okay to not be a 'Squad Goals' type of girl. Okay to make each of your days unapologetically yours.

10

I Am Not Any Man's Personal Porn Star And Neither Are You

Yesterday I came across an Instagram post reading: "A real woman is her man's personal porn star."

Really? I thought. *Really?! Is that what the world has come to?* That the value of a 'real' woman is determined by her sex appeal? By what she can do for her man in the sack? **Beep! Beep! Beep!** The feminist alarms in my head were going off at full volume!

I was half tempted to comment on the guy's post, call him out on how ridiculous it was. Tell him I was personally insulted. That'd teach him! Or, I'd look like that crazy feminist with her hair all frizzy around her head and an 'I Eat Men for Breakfast' t-shirt.

For some reason I didn't comment. I guess I figured I'd save myself the social media argument. I did screen shot it though, with plans to complain about it to my girlfriends over dinner later. But the picture didn't leave my mind. In fact, it haunted me for the rest of that day. (Mind you, I saw this at 5AM, so when I say it bugged me all day, I really mean it!)

29

I kept accidentally opening my gallery, and there it was with its black background and white letters screaming, 'This is your self-worth. This is how you become a real woman.' I couldn't take it anymore. So I took the mature route and commented a face emoji that bore the expression of annoyed/eye-rolling/this-is-dumb/you-are-dumb. It looked something like this (-___-)

Not very mature, I realize this. But I didn't know what to say. Do I comment on it and start an unintelligent argument about how women should be, as Pitbull would say, 'a lady in the street and a freak in the bed'? No. Arguing for the simple fact that women are not defined by their rock star sex abilities would be completely lost on this Instagrammer. He probably wouldn't get it. Or play it off as a harmless joke. And that's what I hate about the internet today.

People are so quick to post dumb stuff without realizing: a.) the consequences, or b.) what they're really saying about others, and more importantly themselves.

They don't think that a picture basically saying a woman's purpose is to serve her man sexually would be pretty insulting. They don't realize that saying something ignorant like that would be a complete turnoff to some women. And they don't realize that the internet is a complete reflection of their character.

The internet today has just become a place of ignorance. With a few clicks, you can lazily search for anything you need without leaving the couch. You can look up a few facts about someone and think you know everything about them. You can write posts and comments instantly, without even having to think. And thus, the mental process is lost. No check-yourself-before-you-wreck-yourself anymore.

If you couldn't click and post an Instagram in a matter of seconds, would things be different? Absolutely. It's the ease of technology, the loss of face-to-face discussion, and the media influences on what we 'should be' that have warped our generation. And I'm sick of it.

So I'm starting to do something about it...with a stale-face emoji, a screenshot, and a shaking fist.

Stay tuned, I might even start wearing my 'I AM A FEMINIST' t-shirt.

11

You Need To Stop Worrying About Who To Love And Start Focusing On What You Love

Life is too damn short. Too. Damn. Short. You're going to face loss and heartbreak, have stomach-dropping-out-of-your-pants moments, giddy-with-butterflies moments, utter despair, and a bunch of jumbled messes in-between. Some days are going to be amazing; some days are going to freaking suck. But bottom line: **this is your life.** And you need to grab ahold of it with your two, bare, semi-calloused, nail-bitten hands **and make something of it.**

Listen. You *will* fall in love at some point. Maybe you already have—lucky for you, no matter how it ended. If you have been in love, you have been blessed with a relationship that has taught you valuable lessons, that has shaped you into a resilient, passionate person, and that has made you believe in one of the most beautiful parts of our human experience. You are lucky.

If you haven't found love, *relax*. Your day will come. You might be wandering around the city and bump into a strange man or woman who catches your eye. It might be as simple as that—embarrassed hellos, exchanged numbers, coffee shop dates, the first, magical, warm kiss—BAM. Love. Or it might be that friend you never expected, whose innocent touch sparked from your hands to your brain and suddenly you thought, *Wow, I freaking love you.*

We don't know how it'll happen, or when, or even why sometimes. But we can't spend our days obsessing over this future, hasn't-even-happened-yet, somewhere-off-in-the-distance relationship because we won't be present in the now. In the everyday monotony, beauty, frustration, confusion, excitement, and glory of the present.

You need to stop worrying about who to love. Stop worrying about if you will find it at the corner book store, at the company party, at the cousin's best friend's wedding. Stop stressing over Tinder matches or Instagram photos or the paralyzing thought, "I am even datable?" Just stop.

When you put your energy and time and constant thoughts into your not-even-real-yet relationship, you're pulling yourself away from what really matters. The everyday life. The happiness, the joy you find in focusing on who you are as a person and what makes you, you.

You need to stop worrying about **who** to love and focus on **what** you love. What motivates you? What makes you passionate? What drives you? Focus on those things. Thrive on those things. Instead of scouring through potential dates' Facebook profiles, lose yourself in a good book. Instead of primping to look 'presentable' for a possible significant other, dress in what makes you *feel good*.

What do you love? Is it art? Sports? Music? Friendships? Sewing? Cooking? Hunting? Reading? Event-planning? Photography? Put your energy, your excitement, your focus, your whole self into those things. Lose yourself in your work, in your hobbies, in your friendships, in you.

And while you're busy becoming a better, whole-r version of yourself, the love you've been searching for will find its way to you. I promise.

<u>12</u>

Read This When You're Feeling Incredibly Small In This Huge, Crazy World

You are small. You are tiny. You are minuscule in a world of millions of people, hundreds of countries, deaths and births, illnesses and natural disasters, celebrations and brokenness.

Your problems will not make a ripple in the pool of life. They will not shift the ground or make volcanoes erupt or alter the cosmos. Your thoughts won't be mind-changing for every living, breathing person on this planet. You are just one lump of cells and organs. Just one human.

But you are significant.

Yes, you are itty-bitty. And yes, you are a speck of the world, but a beautiful speck, an incredible speck constructed of thousands of cells and blood vessels and veins and emotions, swirled and sewn and interlaced together.

You are unique thoughts and emotions, you are laughs and tears and growth spurts and hands that can heal. You are words that can change the direction of another's life. You are kisses to exchange, hugs to give, a heart to share love.

You are broken pieces that will heal together over time. You are a body that lives and teaches strength, a mind that thinks thoughts of positivity and hope.

You are small, yes. But you matter.

Even though your problems are not earth-shattering, even though your voice will not fill the heart of every ear, it may fill one. And that is enough.

You may be a dot on an extremely large, fully detailed map of life, but it is that tiny dot that marks a city, a landmark, something significant. You may feel lost or directionless, scared or without purpose, but your life has meaning.

No matter how small you feel, know this: *if there is one person who cares about you, one person you love, or one life you have touched, that is enough.*

You are enough.

13

You May Feel Broken Right Now, But You Are Not Weak

Today you feel broken. Life has thrown you its toughest hand of cards and you're trying to figure out who you are again, how to move forward in this place of loss.

Your hands feel foreign, your stomach twisted, your heart weighed down. You are unsure of your next step, dizzy and suddenly terrified to stand back up again.

But this is what you do when you are broken. You pick yourself up, piece by piece. You re-learn the strongest parts of yourself and fight until you break through. You drag yourself forward until your limbs can hold your weight, then you learn to stand up, to walk, to smile again.

You hold yourself together with threads, you distract yourself with things and people that occupy your mind and fill the space around you. You walk, you run, you settle into the rhythm of pounding feet on concrete. You comfort yourself with words and soft blankets and laughter until it no longer feels like you're pretending.

You may be broken right now, but it will get better.
You may be broken right now, but you are not weak.

You are never weak. Your head has forgotten its capacity to love, to forgive, to hold memories. Your body has forgotten how to push forward. But you are not this fragile creature that needs to be sheltered, protected, held within a closed fist.

You are not weak. The strongest parts of you are hiding just below the surface, giving you a moment to process. Recharging. The strongest parts of you are building, aligning, bubbling underneath your skin. Waiting for you to believe in them, to set them free.

You are not weak. You do not need to be taken care of. You do not need pity, or gentleness, or someone to carry you, or to hold your hand. You have the strength to stand on your own, the confidence to rebuild, the passion to continue, and the love to forgive.

Though the world may be pulling you down today, though you can't lift the shadow from your eyes, though you are scared of the future, though you are broken, you are not weak.

So close your eyes, take a deep breath, and silently remind yourself of the person you are, of your incredible strength, and begin to piece yourself together again.

14

Read This If You Are Fiercely Independent But Also Ridiculously Emotional

This is what it means to be independent: you make your own decisions, you stand on your own two feet, you pull yourself up when you fall down, and you have your sh*t together.

You have always been this way, always been okay on your own. You have never been afraid to go solo and to trust yourself. And you are continually looking for ways to be even more self-sufficient, to carve your own life path, to do what you want.

But you also love. And love terribly, beautifully, fully. You love with a passion that's sickening. A consuming, knotting, mess of emotion that interweaves you with another person. A love that twists your feelings, throws you upside-down, and makes you put your faith and stubbornness and fiercely-independent self in the hands of this other person.

Because of this, you live in a constant state of tension.

There are two things you want—to be your own person and to love—but you want them just as equally. You crave that sense of self, the ability to not have to depend on anyone else for the life you want. But when you love, you mesh your life with another person's. Willingly. Happily. The path you have set for yourself becomes tangled with that person's. And this both thrills and terrifies you.

Your world then becomes an inner battle. You quiet your stubborn mind and give into love. You find yourself curling into this person's lap like a puppy, craving his touch, his kiss. Falling. You become the woman that confides in a man, the woman that leans on a man when she's feeling lost, the woman that thinks of this man equally, if not before, herself. This is beautiful. This is love.

But then you suddenly balk. You feel weak, dependent, breakable. You have become the woman that let a man in, who trusted him, who can easily be crushed by the same hands that touch her. So you swing to the other side. You pull away. You spend time alone, just recharging, remembering that sense of self. Letting go.

Neither side makes you fully happy. Neither side leaves you feeling complete. You cannot seem to find a balance because you crave both things so equally. And so you live in this place of tension—what you want and who you are, what you are becoming and yet so scared to be.

You are an independent woman. A woman with a strong heart and passionate soul. You cannot let go of that part of you, the part that decides for herself, finds strength in her ability to stand alone. Yet you cannot be afraid to love. You cannot be afraid to embrace that ridiculously emotional side of you, the side that blends your strength with your passion. The side that makes you whole.

You are not complete without both—without the strength you carry, without the tears and words and kisses you freely give. You are a strong woman. You are an emotional woman. You are a perfect mix of both.

15

To The Woman Who Doesn't Sleep Around, This Is For You

You don't take guys home. You don't go to the bars with intentions. You don't Netflix and Chill. And you definitely don't see sex as something casual.

You are a woman who doesn't sleep around. This is how you've defined yourself. This is the legacy you lead and the strength you carry, even when it doesn't feel like it. You are admired, just so you know.

You are the type of woman who sees sex as something beautiful, something special, maybe even something sacred. Sex, you believe, should be shared between you and select person(s). Maybe with a deep, unexplainable connection. Maybe with love. Maybe with marriage. Regardless, you hold yourself, and men, to a higher standard. You love deeply. You know what you deserve and don't settle for anything less. And that makes you powerful.

We live in a world where it's okay to sleep around, okay to have sexual freedom, okay to have multiple partners. All these things are awesome for women—to have the ability, the choice, the control of our own bodies and decisions. But this isn't for every single woman. You are a woman, a Feminist who stands for the purity of her own body. You don't find sex with multiple men liberating or empowering. And that is absofreakinglutely okay.

You are not crazy. Not weird. Not a flirt, tease, prude, stuck-up, trying to be 'better' than anyone, or any other negative words the world wants to label you with. You are a woman who embraces her sexuality as much as any other woman. You are just selective about who you give your body to.

You're going to face opposition. You're going to meet women who will judge you and men who will chastise you. You will have days when you're not sure if you'll ever find your 'right' guy. (You will.) You'll have moments when you're challenged to hold to your beliefs, when you'll question if you should change who you are and just be flippant with sex. But stay strong. There is a world of women out there, just like you. You are loved. You are not alone.

16

It's Never Too Late To Start Over

It's never too late to start over. To hit the pause button. Breathe. Then begin again.

You don't need to lose yourself in the shuffle, get caught up in your mistakes and your fears and your anxieties. You don't have to hold onto your anger or your sadness and carry it with you in a little jar. You are more than a little jar, waiting to be filled by unsatisfying things—material things, superficial love, addictions and vices and so many other negatives that leave you feeling emptier than before. You are more than that little jar you feel defines the person you are, so much so that you try to fit yourself in its glass walls, try to keep contained within the edges and not overflow.

Life is imperfect. It's beautiful and complicated and burdensome and messy. And you are a part of it, a part that grows and changes and laughs and loves and gets broken and comes back together. But there will never be a time when you can't just step back and start all over.

There is no rewind, but you can always restart, let go. Let go of the toxic friends, of the urge to gossip, of the anxieties over what he said and she said, of the worry you feel over a future you cannot control. Let go. It's never too late to put down that jar of you're carrying and pull yourself out of it. Grab your legs and arms and brain and heart and soul and reconstruct them back into the self you're supposed to be. Reshape. Remold. Reconnect. And begin again.

You are not supposed to be this static person, this person you've always been and always will be. The world is continually shifting, and you are continually moving within it, in whatever direction you want. If you don't like that direction, turn. Don't turn back. Don't turn around. Just turn. Right. Left. Diagonal. Cut across the grass. Take a back road.

It's never too late to spin things around for the better. To leave what's been broken and acknowledge that you can't put it back together exactly how it was. To smile at the things you cannot replace, cannot fix, cannot make perfect. Nothing is perfect. You are not perfect. So don't drag around that little jar, the transparent jar of your imperfections for the world to see, for you to see as a constant reminder of the ways you've failed. Forget the jar. Forget how you've always been defined by it and define yourself by something new. Throw it down. Shatter it. Watch it fall and break and crush into a thousand tiny pieces and celebrate that change hurts, and that growth sucks. But now you are free falling, and it is terrifying, but terribly freeing.

Then start over. Begin again. All at once, or piece by piece. Start with the little things. Then be patient as you begin again, becoming new, becoming yourself.

17

I Will Never Be An 'IDGAF' Type Of Girl

I love being a woman. I love rocking heels and dresses, sweatpants and messy buns, rings and makeup and gym shoes and baseball caps and lipstick. Being a woman is fun. It's challenging and exciting and frustrating and wonderful.

But there is one type of woman I will never be: one with a flippant attitude towards love and sex and relationships. Don't get me wrong, I admire the hell out of these types of ladies. They are passionate and strong and bold and courageous. But I can't, and will never be, an 'IDGAF' type of girl.

I have too much heart, to a flaw. In my friendships, I care so incredibly. When I love, I fall completely, fully, fearlessly. And when my heart is broken, I forgive, let go, and continue loving because that is who I am. Who I'll always be.

It is not out of weakness. In fact, sometimes I feel that my ability to love is my greatest strength. It is not because I'm lovesick or fragile or terrified to lose the people and memories in my life. But it is because I cannot be one of those people who turns off the faucet, who can just stop caring with the click of a button.

I am passionate, emotional, stubborn, and driven. I care about the work I do, the words I write, the choices I make, the friendships I have, and the men I choose to love. And in the wake of all of these things, no matter the outcome, I still care. I carry the memories in my back pocket. I use them to become even stronger, to discover myself again, to be an even better person.

I am not a girl with a 'f*ck it' attitude. I cannot say 'f*ck' it to love, 'f*ck it' to sex, 'f*ck it' to friendships, 'f*ck it' to the person I am and have been my entire life.

I care too much. That has always been the one thing that does me in. I fight for relationships and I can't walk away from friendships because I don't want to lose the people that I've had in my life. I can't just let things blow up and slowly sizzle out, like a candle burning to the quick. I can't just watch what once meant everything to me drift to nothingness, become unimportant. I can't be passive, letting people and memories and things I care about slip out of my grasp. I can't just sit there, throw my hands up, and say 'oh well,' say 'f*ck it.' Because I am, and always will be, a fighter. Even if it's a battle I've already lost.

Sometimes I wish I could be that 'IDGAF' type of girl. The girl that speaks brutal truths without caring if they'll hurt people around her. Who calls people out on their sh*t, even if it ends up backfiring. Those type of girls have always impressed me. They don't tip-toe around people's crap. They live fearlessly and openly. They know how to stand up; they know when enough's enough. And they know how to purge the sh*t that brings them down out of their lives. For good.

I'm strong in my own ways, but I'm also sensitive. I think about what other people feel, because I feel everything so deeply. But sometimes I wish I didn't. Sometimes I wish I could say *I'm done* and turn around, turn away, cut people off, be flippant, be free.

But that's just not me.

So I'll choose my words intentionally. I'll speak my honesty carefully. And I'll love, even foolishly. Because that's the type of girl I am.

I will always give a f*ck.

18

The Truth About Being A Strong Woman

This is what an anonymous man wrote to me just the other day: *Being strong is not rewarded. Women are expected to be vulnerable. Being strong means that you're inevitably bitter or jaded about something, and that's just not attractive.*

Here is what being a strong woman means to me: It means standing up for myself. It means that I am a fully-functioning human, one who is independent and able to do things for herself. It means that I have opinions and beliefs that I stand for, and that I do not settle for less.

It doesn't mean that I don't ask for help. I do (often). Asking for help doesn't mean I'm weak, it means I'm able to acknowledge that I'm not a super woman, and that I'm going to need other people sometimes.

Being strong doesn't mean that I close myself off from others and act like I'm better than them. (Actually, I'm always striving to be better, live better, love better, which is about *me* rather than anyone else.) It doesn't mean that I force my beliefs down other people's throats, or judge them for how they think. It doesn't mean that I'm 'inevitably bitter or jaded.' In fact, a strong woman is a woman who loves herself and her world and is therefore positive, loving, and self-assured.

To be a strong woman simply means that I am grounded and confident in who I am.

I read this man's comment. Then read it again. And resisted the incredible urge to reply and start a back-and-forth battle via computer screens that would end up going nowhere. But even after a few days, this comment has stayed with me.

See, this is the misconception about strong women: that we are difficult to love. But in all reality, it's the complete opposite. **Strong women are the best women to love.** We are the women with fierce compassion. We know who we are and we are not afraid to embrace that. **We love whole-heartedly because we love ourselves.** And we are not only looking to better ourselves, but our partners, our worlds. If you're a man that's intimidated by a strong woman, perhaps it is because you know this woman will push you to be better, will make you see the world differently, will challenge you.

Another misconception about strong women is that we're incapable of being vulnerable. The funny thing is: **to be strong, you first have to be vulnerable.** You have to look yourself straight in the eye and acknowledge all the parts of yourself that need improvement, all the parts of you that you try to hide behind a smiling face.

Vulnerability means being brutally honest with yourself; it means setting aside your pride and being open with someone and letting them in. Do not mistake independence and strength with an inability to let someone in. A woman that is confident with herself is a woman that will face love straight on. **She is a woman that can be vulnerable in a relationship because she knows who she is.** And she will let her significant other discover that person by peeling back those layers, together.

The truth about being a strong woman is that the world sees us as a threat. We're just 'too much,' 'too intimidating,' too 'jaded' and 'miserable' and 'bitter'. But we are none of those things. We are women with backbones. Women who aren't afraid to be proud of ourselves in a world that might not always support us. Women who know the value of our vulnerability, our passion, our strength. And women who will fight any anonymous man who dares to say we should be any other way.

Thought Catalog, it's a website.
www.thoughtcatalog.com

Social
facebook.com/thoughtcatalog
twitter.com/thoughtcatalog
tumblr.com/thoughtcatalog

Corporate
www.thought.is

Made in the USA
Monee, IL
02 January 2021

56129118R00042